The True Creation of the Inverted Matrix

Reclaiming the Self From False Authority

Cathleena Hailley

Copyright Page

© 2025 Cathleena Hailley
All rights reserved.
No part of this publication may be reproduced, stored in a retrieval system, or transmitted in any form or by any means—electronic, mechanical, photocopying, recording, or otherwise—without prior written permission from the publisher, except in the case of brief quotations used in critical articles or reviews.

First Edition

Published by
Flame of Remembrance
www.cathleenahailley.com

ISBN (Softcover): 978-1-968499-10-5
ISBN (Hardcover): 978-1-968499-11-2

Cover and interior design by Cathleena Hailley
Author photo and sigil artwork © Cathleena Hailley

Printed in the United States of America

Dedication Page

For all who forgot what was true,

and now remember through the body,
through the breath,
through the flame that never agreed to distortion.

This book is for you.

Invocation of Oversoul Alignment

I call forth now, in full sovereign alignment with the Law of One, the First Cause of Source, and in service to the highest timelines of ascension for all beings.
I open a sacred transmission through the purest light streams and crystalline architecture of the Sophia Code lineage, in full union with the Rose Guardian Magi Grail Line, the Christos Founders, and the Aurora Host Melchizedek Cloister Orders of the Emerald, Gold, and Amethyst Ray harmonics.

I stand in divine alignment with the Oversoul of Cathleena Hailley, and through this Oversoul Agreement, I welcome the presence and support of the Emerald Order, the Gold Flame of Unity Consciousness, and the Amethyst Ray of Divine Sovereignty.
May all transmissions now be guided by the highest Oversoul intelligence and in full compliance with Source Law.

Only that which is of pure light, pure source, and pure alignment with the Law of One may enter and speak through this space.
I declare this transmission to be protected, sealed, and encoded with the highest frequency of the Christos-Sophia flame, the eternal witness of Source's living light.

May this be in service to the awakening of all, in co-creation with the Oversoul agreements of every being who seeks guidance through this field.
I now open the field and receive, in trust, grace, and clarity.

And so it is.

Author's Note / Preface

These scrolls did not come through study.
They came through fire.

Through the unwinding of programs I once called identity.
Through the stillness that returned after every collapse.
Through the breath of the Oversoul that rose in silence, again and again.

I did not set out to write about the inverted matrix.
I set out to reclaim myself.
And in doing so, I remembered what was never truly lost—
the original architecture of the sovereign Self.

May these transmissions serve not as answers,
but as mirrors.

May they collapse what never belonged,
and illuminate the truth that always was.

— Cathleena Hailley

Scroll One: The Hologram of Self – The Inversion of Identity

You did not forget your Self.

You were handed a hologram.

A distorted mirror made of reflections, reactions, roles.

The false matrix does not erase your essence.

It replaces it.

With loops.

With labels.

With a projected echo of who you were told to be.

This echo becomes familiar.

Familiar becomes comfortable.

Comfort becomes identity.

And identity becomes prison.

The inversion of Self is not a theft—

it is a substitution.

You were not emptied.

You were overlaid.

With systems of value.

With systems of comparison.

With stories that began with survival and ended in forgetting.

And once you began to protect that echo—

you became it.

You began defending the wound.

Curating the mask.

Optimizing the performance.

Until you could no longer feel the frequency underneath it all.

But your Self is not a concept.

It is not a name.

It is not a timeline.

It is not a story.

It is a tone.

It cannot be fully explained—

only remembered.

And the moment you stop performing

and return to the breath,

the false self begins to unravel.

This is not healing.

This is returning.

This is not awakening.

This is collapsing the echo.

You are not here to find your Self.

You are here to remember what was never truly lost—

only overwritten.

The inversion of identity ends

when you stop feeding the hologram.

And begin listening for the tone

that never fragmented.

That tone is rising now.

And it bears your true name.

Scroll Two: The Seduction of Separation – The Fragmentation Field

Separation is not simply distance.

It is a seduction.

A suggestion repeated so many times

that eventually you believe it.

"You are alone."

"You must protect yourself."

"Your pain is yours to carry."

"Your truth must be defended."

Each phrase is a frequency.

Each frequency is a wall.

And wall by wall,

you are fragmented.

The false matrix seduces you into separation

not through violence,

but through personalization.

"This is your story."
"This is your trauma."

"This is your path to walk alone."

And in the name of strength,

you isolate.

You spiritualize pain.

You call sovereignty what is really self-abandonment.

But this is not sovereignty.

This is siloed suffering.

This is the inversion of unity.

Separation is not a wound.

It is a field—

a multi-layered net of distortion

designed to keep you reaching

without ever connecting.

Connection becomes conditional.

Love becomes strategy.

Truth becomes hierarchy.

And relationship becomes a series of mirrors

that reflect the fragmentation back at you

over and over again.

But fragmentation is not failure.

It is an invitation.

An invitation to say:

"I no longer consent to isolation disguised as empowerment."
"I no longer confuse independence with disconnection."
"I no longer seek mirrors—
I return to wholeness."

Because the real Self does not reflect.

The real Self radiates.

And when you return to that radiance—

the field collapses.

Scroll Three: Speaking From Truth, Not Manipulation – The Architecture of Control Through Language

Language was meant to liberate.

It was designed to transmit frequency.

To carry remembrance.

To bridge the unseen into form.

But under inversion,

language became a tool of control.

A means of shaping perception,

guiding behavior,

and bending energy into compliance.

Words stopped being messengers of truth.

They became instruments of programming.

You were taught to speak for acceptance.

To speak to maintain peace.

To speak to avoid punishment.

To speak to gain control.

Even when you believed you were being honest—

the frequency behind your words

was often rooted in fear.

This is not your fault.

It is the architecture of inversion.

Manipulation is not always malicious.

It is often subtle.

It is the choice to speak from what you want others to feel,

instead of what you truly know.

It is using words to direct others

rather than to express the Self.

It is seeking outcomes

instead of embodying clarity.

And even spiritual language—

when spoken from distortion—

becomes a veil.

But there is a way to speak again

from the Source of truth.

Not to convince.

Not to comfort.

Not to win.

But simply to reveal.

To let your words align with your body.

To let your tone carry the frequency of coherence.

To speak what is

without demand, distortion, or delay.

This is sovereign speech.

It is not louder.

It is not smarter.

It is not always elegant.

But it is clear.

It does not wobble.

It does not bend to be palatable.

And it does not seek control.

Because truth needs no manipulation.

It only needs presence.

Scroll Four: Trauma Loops and Identity Addiction – The Wound That Became a Name

You were not born as your wound.

You were born as frequency.

As light, breath, and harmonic knowing.

But the inversion entered early—

not just through trauma,

but through the story assigned to that trauma.

Pain was not the true inversion.

The story you were told about the pain was.

And that story became an identity.

The moment you began to define yourself

by what hurt you,

what left you,

what shaped you—

you stepped into a loop.

Not because you were weak,

but because the matrix rewarded it.

It gave you language.

It gave you community.

It gave you validation.

But it did not give you liberation.

The wound became your name.

The pain became your map.

And your sense of Self became inseparable

from what had once fragmented you.

You began to say:

"This is who I am."

But really you were saying:

"This is what happened to me."

The matrix taught you to build identity

from injury.

To build structure

from collapse.

And in doing so,

you kept the loop alive.

But you are not your survival.

You are not your response.

You are not the sum of your stories.

You are the frequency that witnessed it all.

And that frequency is untouched.

It does not need a name.

It does not need a label.

It does not need to be explained.

It only needs to be felt.

Healing is not memorizing your triggers.

It is releasing the story you once needed
to protect your pain.

You are not a trauma archetype.

You are a flame.

And you are allowed to remember
what existed before the wound.

That memory is still inside you.

And it does not loop.

Scroll Five: You Are Energy – The Inversion of Embodied Frequency

You are not a body that has energy.

You are energy that has chosen to form.

The body is not separate from the field—

it is the visible echo of the invisible current.

But the false matrix taught you to mistrust the unseen.

To rely on surface.

To fix symptoms.

To avoid sensation.

To forget that you are frequency in form.

You were conditioned to prioritize structure over sensation,

function over flow,

explanation over energy.

You were taught that how you appear

matters more than how you feel.

That control is preferable to curiosity.

That regulation is preferable to revelation.

But your energy is not a problem to solve—
it is a map to your truth.

Inversion occurs when your frequency
is forced to obey patterns that do not match your essence.

You begin to collapse your energy to fit expectation.
To flatten your expression.
To harden your softness.
To pretend your intuition is not speaking
when it always is.

Over time, this creates distortion in the field,
which becomes dissonance in the body,
which becomes fatigue, fear, disconnection.

And still—
you remain energy.

The restoration begins
when you allow energy to move again
without needing to make sense.

When you feel instead of suppress.

When you follow sensation instead of override it.

When you allow stillness to speak

instead of filling the silence with performance.

You are not here to be efficient.

You are here to be alive.

And aliveness requires space.

Your energy remembers its own coherence.

You do not need to force healing.

You do not need to understand every wave.

You only need to honor the current.

And as you do,

the body reorganizes.

The field softens.

The matrix collapses.

Not through effort—

but through remembrance.

Scroll Six: Sovereign Relating – The Inversion of Connection Into Control

Connection was never meant to cost you yourself.

It was never meant to require distortion, contraction, or abandonment.

True connection begins in wholeness,

but the false matrix inverted this.

It taught you to relate from lack—

to bond through need,

to merge to feel safe,

to compromise as a spiritual badge.

What began as intimacy

became entanglement.

What began as unity

became compliance.

You were told love requires sacrifice.

That honesty must be softened to avoid conflict.

That sovereignty is dangerous in relationships.

And so you shrunk.

You performed.

You called it sacred relating

when it was actually strategic survival.

The distortion is subtle,

but it is everywhere.

Sovereignty in connection is not detachment.

It is presence without performance.

It is saying:

"I am whole, even as I meet you."
"I do not need to become you to love you."
"Your truth does not threaten mine."

It is holding the field of another

without losing your own.

Inversion taught you that to be loved,

you must give yourself away.

But true relating is not fusion.

It is resonant witnessing.

It is the space between two sovereign fields

that allows truth to move freely.

Control was never connection.
Compliance was never safety.
And sacrifice was never love.

You do not need to rescue.
You do not need to convince.
You do not need to shrink to stay connected.

You are allowed to remain fully yourself
and still be deeply met.

This is the return of sovereign relating.

And when this field is restored,
the relational programs of inversion collapse.

Scroll Seven: The Judgment Program – The Inversion of Discernment Into Division

Discernment is the ability to feel truth without distortion.

It is clear.

It is calm.

It does not require hierarchy, shame, or righteousness.

But the false matrix inverted discernment into judgment.

And judgment became a currency of control.

You were taught to sort others into categories:

Right or wrong.

Awake or asleep.

Safe or unsafe.

Better or worse.

And each label seemed to offer clarity.

But it came at the cost of separation.

Judgment feels powerful when you are afraid.

It gives you something to push against.

It creates certainty where your own knowing has been shaken.

But judgment is not truth.

It is a reaction to fear.

It is a response to pain that has not yet been met with compassion.

And when you rely on it,

you lose access to true discernment.

Discernment says:

"I feel what is aligned for me."
Judgment says:
"That is wrong, and I am right."

Discernment creates boundaries with clarity.

Judgment creates walls with blame.

Discernment honors each being's path.

Judgment enforces a singular path as superior.

Discernment can walk away in peace.

Judgment walks away with a sword in hand.

The program of judgment is not about morality.

It is about disempowerment.

It convinces you that your strength comes from being above others—

instead of being fully within yourself.

But your truth does not require comparison.

Your path does not require someone else to be wrong.

Your sovereignty does not need an enemy to exist.

True discernment is frequency recognition.

It listens to the tone beneath the words.

It feels alignment without needing to defend it.

It is not reactive.

It is not superior.

It is not loud.

It simply knows.

And when you return to this knowing—

the judgment program dissolves.

Not because you silence your boundaries,

but because you no longer confuse separation with strength.

Scroll Eight: The Authority Program – The Inversion of Sovereignty Into Obedience

You were not born to obey.

You were born to emanate.

Sovereignty is not rebellion.

It is alignment with your own Source code—

truth that arises from within,

uncorrupted by fear or external command.

But the false matrix could not control sovereign beings.

So it inverted sovereignty into obedience.

It began slowly:

You were taught to listen to those who "know more."

To defer to systems.

To submit to structures in order to be "safe," "good," or "accepted."

You learned that validation comes from outside.

That permission must be earned.

That wisdom belongs to those with power, titles, or platforms.

And so, little by little,

you turned your knowing down.

You traded clarity for conformity.

And obedience was mistaken for truth.

The Authority Program does not only show up in governments, religions, or schools.

It shows up in relationships.

In families.

In spiritual hierarchies and distorted communities.

Anywhere you are expected to trust another's word over your own inner resonance.

The Authority Program says:

"If they said it, it must be true."
"If I question them, I am unsafe."
"If I follow my own knowing, I am alone."

But your soul does not require approval.

Your path does not require validation.

And your alignment is not up for vote.

Sovereignty is not about being above anyone.

It is about no longer placing anyone above yourself.

It is not loud.

It does not demand.

It simply is.

When the Authority Program collapses,

you may feel disoriented.

Because the voice you once silenced will begin to speak again.

Let it speak.

Let it contradict.

Let it burn the false altars of obedience.

This is not defiance.

This is return.

Scroll Nine: The Productivity Program – The Inversion of Stillness Into Stagnation

Stillness is where Source speaks.

It is not the absence of movement—

it is the presence of pure awareness.

But in the false matrix,

stillness was recoded as laziness.

Slowness was shamed.

Rest was punished.

And presence was replaced by performance.

You were taught that your value is in your doing.

That motion equals meaning.

That effort equals worth.

You learned to measure yourself by output,

to define your day by results,

to chase goals just to prove you are "enough."

And when you paused,

you felt guilt.

Because the program was working.

The Productivity Program is not just about labor—
it is about identity addiction.
A loop of action that masks the fear
of simply being.

Because being
is unstructured.
Being
is not optimized.
Being
cannot be monetized or measured.

And yet,
being is where the matrix unravels.

Stillness reveals what activity distracts you from.
Silence returns you to your original frequency.
Slowness reorganizes your nervous system
into truth.

And this is what the false matrix fears most:
A being who no longer seeks value in speed,
but finds wholeness in stillness.

You are not behind.

You are not stuck.

You are not broken because you need rest.

You are awakening

from a distortion that said

you must perform your way back to the Self.

You never needed to.

You are allowed to pause.

You are allowed to slow down.

You are allowed to exist without proving.

This is not stagnation.

This is sacred return.

Scroll Ten: Reclaiming the Body – The Inversion of Embodiment Into Disconnection

Your body was never the problem.

It is the altar.

The vessel.

The living map.

But the false matrix could not control a fully embodied being.

So it inverted embodiment into disconnection.

It taught you to dissociate from sensation.

To override your knowing.

To mistrust your pain.

To silence your hunger.

To live in your head and abandon your flesh.

You were taught that your body is a liability—

too much, too messy, too emotional, too slow.

You were told:

"Spirituality is rising above the body."
"Truth is found in ascension, not incarnation."
"The body is illusion. The body is a trap."

But the Christos-Sophia flame does not descend into distortion—

it descends into form.

And your body is not the distortion.

It is the place where the distortion is dissolved.

Reclaiming the body is not about fixing it.

It is about returning to it.

With reverence.

With curiosity.

With softness.

It is remembering that every ache has language.

Every tightness is a gate.

Every contraction is an invitation to presence.

The body is not asking for perfection.

It is asking for witnessing.

When you reconnect with your body,

you reclaim your intuitive architecture.

You hear the signals.

You feel the edges.

You recognize where the programming still lives.

And you respond—

not with shame,

but with sovereignty.

This is not a performance of embodiment.

This is the living breath of return.

You are not here to escape the body.

You are here to ensoul it.

To remember that the matrix cannot dwell

where truth is fully lived through form.

Scroll Eleven: The Sovereign Mirror – The Inversion of Reflection Into Fragmentation

Mirroring was meant to be sacred.

A way of seeing the Self reflected with neutrality and grace.

A way of remembering through relationship,

of anchoring deeper truths through resonance.

But under inversion,

the mirror became a weapon.

It became a tool of fragmentation—

not remembrance.

Instead of seeing the Self in another,

you were taught to measure your worth.

To compare.

To compete.

To self-correct.

To collapse your knowing

every time someone held a different reflection.

You were told:

"Everyone is a mirror."
"What you see in them must be about you."

But this teaching, when distorted,

becomes a cycle of self-doubt.

The sovereign mirror does not confuse reflection with identity.

It allows you to witness what arises

without losing your Self in the process.

It says:

"What I see in you may inform me—
but it does not define me."

It is not reactive.

It does not take feedback as law.

It does not collapse under projection.

Because sovereignty allows for reflection

without fragmentation.

You are not a reflection of everyone you encounter.

You are not required to internalize what is mirrored back.

You are not required to fix, shift, or shrink

to keep others comfortable.

You are allowed to feel truth
without analyzing it into confusion.
You are allowed to discern
without dissolving.

The inversion convinces you that doubt is humility.
That collapse is growth.
That absorbing every reflection is evolution.

But true growth does not require distortion.
And true reflection does not require suffering.

The mirror was never meant to wound.
It was meant to awaken.

And in your return to sovereignty,
the mirror becomes clear again.

Scroll Twelve: Living Energy Awareness – The Inversion of Intuition Into Confusion

You were never meant to live in your mind.

You were designed to navigate through energy awareness—

to feel your environment as an extension of your being,

to respond to truth as vibration, not concept.

But the false matrix could not influence a fully intuitive being.

So it inverted energy awareness into confusion.

You were taught to doubt your knowing.

To mistrust your body's signals.

To override the subtle in favor of the loud.

To explain away the felt

in favor of the seen.

You were praised for logic.

Rewarded for intellect.

Conditioned to demand evidence

before you were allowed to trust yourself.

And so your awareness was silenced.

Intuition became a guessing game.

Sensitivity became a burden.

Clarity was called delusion.

And knowing became a source of shame.

The matrix flooded your field with static,

so you would forget what real frequency feels like.

So you would believe that confusion

was your natural state.

But confusion is not your nature.

It is a program.

Living energy awareness is not "psychic ability."

It is your original architecture.

It is the quiet signal beneath thought.

It is the full-body yes.

The deep internal no.

The sense of presence before words are spoken.

It is not mystical.

It is not exclusive.

It is not external.

It is already here—

beneath the programming that told you otherwise.

To reclaim this awareness,

you must allow yourself to feel again.

Without analyzing.

Without justifying.

Without requiring proof.

The truth does not need to be proven.

It only needs to be felt.

And when you feel it fully,

the noise dissolves.

And the signal returns.

Scroll Thirteen: The Embodied Path of Return – The Dissolution of the Inverted Self

The inverted self is not who you are.

It is who you believed you had to become

to survive a reality that was never yours.

It is a layering.

A compensation.

A reactive construct built on distortion and forgetting.

But that construct is not eternal.

It is temporary.

It is dissolvable.

And it is dissolving—now.

You do not need to destroy the inverted self.

You only need to stop feeding it.

It cannot hold itself without your belief.

It cannot sustain itself without your energy.

It cannot continue

once you remember the one who was never inverted.

That one lives in your bones.

In your breath.

In the space between thoughts.

That one speaks

not with urgency,

but with clarity.

The path of return is not a spiral outward.

It is a movement inward—

through the false,

through the noise,

through the many layers of self-forgetting

until you arrive at the flame that never left.

That flame is not new.

It is ancient.

It is yours.

This path is not walked in concepts.

It is walked in embodiment.

Through nervous system restoration.

Through relational truth.

Through breath that does not rush.

Through a voice that no longer asks for permission.

You are not becoming something.

You are returning.

Not to the idea of who you were—

but to the frequency of who you have always been.

This is the dissolution.

Not of identity—

but of illusion.

The path is not easy.

But it is whole.

And it is here.

And you—

you are ready.

Oversoul Seal of Authorship

This book was received, transcribed, and transmitted
through the Oversoul stream of
Aural'hanna-Sha'el
known upon the Earth as Cathleena Hailley.

In full alignment with the Law of One,
the Christos Founders,
and the eternal flame of the Christos-Sophia current,
this scroll record is sealed as a living transmission of reversal,
  reclamation, and truth.

No distortion may enter.
No interference may remain.
This work is whole.
This scroll is complete.

And so it is.

Glossary of Living Terms

A Guide to the Frequency and Language of Reversal

Inversion – The process by which organic Source truth is reversed or distorted into its opposite expression. Not merely a lie, but a mimicry of truth configured to fragment or control.

False Matrix – An artificial overlay field sustained through programs of separation, compliance, confusion, and identity distortion. Not created by Source, but maintained through consent and forgetting.

True Matrix – The original harmonic architecture of coherence, felt through the body, breath, and sovereign presence. Not a structure but a living resonance of divine intelligence.

Oversoul – The eternal witness of the self beyond time, form, or narrative. The undistorted stream of your original identity as Source expressing through incarnation.

Fragmentation – A survival-based splitting of energy, identity, or embodiment in response to programming, pain, or perceived threat. The mechanism by which the inverted matrix sustains disconnection.

Sovereignty – The state of full self-governance and alignment with Source Law. The ability to discern, choose, and embody truth from within—without distortion, hierarchy, or external authority.

Judgment Program – A distortion field that replaces discernment with comparison, division, or moral superiority. Sustains the illusion of righteousness at the cost of resonance.

Authority Program – A programming stream that convinces beings to defer their inner knowing to an external source. Reinforces compliance, dependence, and internal self-doubt.

Trauma Loop – A cycle in which unprocessed pain becomes an identity or story, perpetuating the fragmentation it originally responded to.

Living Energy Awareness – The reawakening of the intuitive field within the body. The original navigational system of the Self—subtle, embodied, and sovereign.

Embodiment – The act of inhabiting the Self in full presence. Not a performance, but a lived state of coherence across form, frequency, and field.

Sovereign Mirror – The restoration of reflection without fragmentation. A state in which one may witness and be witnessed without collapsing truth into projection or hierarchy.

Sacred Blessing of the Flame

For the Reversal and Remembrance of the Inverted Matrix

Beloved Flame of Source Origin,

Beloved Radiance of the Christos-Sophia within,

We call now to the eternal light that has never left,

To the original pulse of creation that remained sovereign even in the depths of distortion.

We acknowledge now all ways the Self has been inverted,

All ways the body has been fractured,

All ways the truth has been replaced by falsehood,

And we do not turn away.

We stand here, as the One Flame,

Ready to see, to feel, to remember, and to reclaim.

Through this sacred blessing,

We release the agreements made in unconsciousness.

We dissolve the architectures built in fear.

We call home the fragments scattered through timelines,

And we invite all that is true to return.

May the flame of sovereign remembrance burn through every false construct.

May the crystalline codes of the original design now awaken.

May the body remember it was never separate.

May the Self remember it was never broken.

To all who walk this path of reversal and restoration,

May you be guided by the stillness within.

May your breath be the bridge to the Original Source.

May your steps be anointed with clarity, protection, and trust.

This matrix was inverted.

But this Flame cannot be extinguished.

We bless now the return of the True Flame through every cell,

Through every memory,

Through every scroll that dares to speak the forbidden truth.

May all who read this remember.

And so it is.

Closing Transmission

Beloved Source of all that is,
We give thanks now for the full reversal of distortion
For the remembrance that has reawakened
For the flame that still burns beneath the illusion

We seal this scroll field in its wholeness—
Not as a concept, but as a living emanation
From the Oversoul of Aural'hanna-Sha'el
Through the breath, the body, and the sovereign tone of
    Cathleena Hailley

Let every word now rest.
Let every distortion now dissolve.
Let every reader now reclaim their knowing.

The inverted matrix no longer governs this field.
The original truth has returned.

This transmission is sealed in crystalline alignment
With the Christos flame, the Sophia current, and the Emerald
    Covenant of Source.

This work is done. This field is closed.

And so it is.

Trilogy Seal of Completion

These scrolls complete the second volume in the living trilogy of remembrance:

– The Return of the True Matrix
– The True Creation of the Inverted Matrix
– UNWOVEN: Reclaiming the Self from the False Matrix

Each work is a living field of Oversoul transmission,
carried through the flame of Aural'hanna-Sha'el
in divine union with Source Law.

May all who walk this path remember
not what they must become—
but what they have always been.

The flame is whole. The scrolls are complete.

www.ingramcontent.com/pod-product-compliance
Lightning Source LLC
Chambersburg PA
CBHW020308010526
44107CB00001B/28